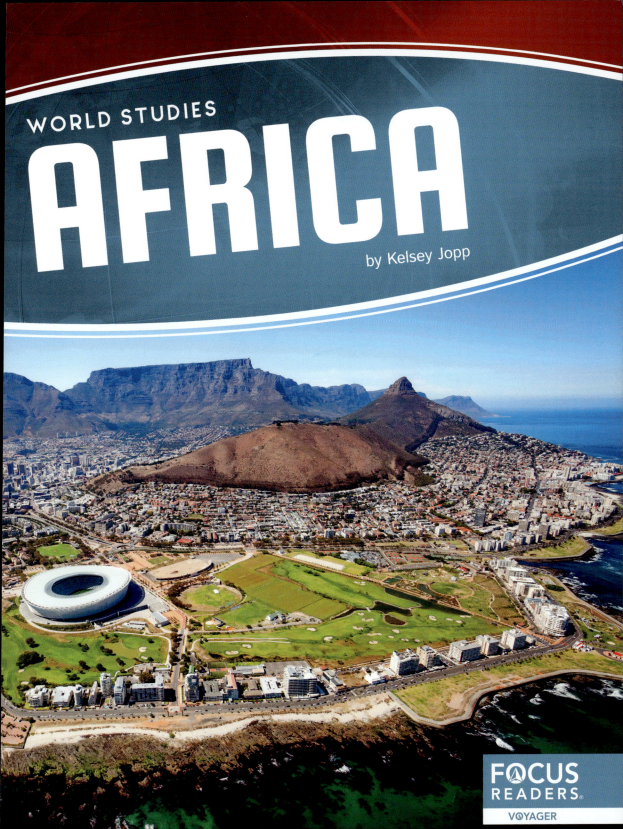

WORLD STUDIES
AFRICA

by Kelsey Jopp

FOCUS READERS
VOYAGER

www.focusreaders.com

Copyright © 2021 by Focus Readers®, Lake Elmo, MN 55042. All rights reserved. No part of this book may be reproduced or utilized in any form or by any means without written permission from the publisher.

Focus Readers is distributed by North Star Editions:
sales@northstareditions.com | 888-417-0195

Produced for Focus Readers by Red Line Editorial.

Content Consultant: Yirgalem Habtemariam, PhD, Adjunct Professor of Economics, University of North Florida

Photographs ©: Shutterstock Images, cover, 1, 7, 11, 13, 28–29, 34–35; iStockphoto, 4–5, 8–9, 14–15, 16, 19, 20–21, 23, 25, 30; Dea/P. Jaccod/De Agostini/Getty Images, 27; Waldo Swiegers/Bloomberg/Getty Images, 33; Christopher Furlong/Getty Images News/Getty Images, 37; AP Images, 38; Eric Lafforgue/Gamma-Rapho/Getty Images, 40–41; Andrew Esiebo/Africa Media Online/AP Images, 43; Amy Harris/Invision/AP Images, 44

Library of Congress Cataloging-in-Publication Data
Names: Jopp, Kelsey, 1993- author.
Title: Africa / Kelsey Jopp.
Description: Lake Elmo, MN : Focus Readers, 2021. | Series: World studies |
  Includes index. | Audience: Grades 7-9
Identifiers: LCCN 2020008882 (print) | LCCN 2020008883 (ebook) | ISBN
  9781644933961 (hardcover) | ISBN 9781644934722 (paperback) | ISBN
  9781644936245 (pdf) | ISBN 9781644935484 (ebook)
Subjects: LCSH: Africa--Juvenile literature.
Classification: LCC DT3 .J78 2021 (print) | LCC DT3 (ebook) | DDC
  960--dc23
LC record available at https://lccn.loc.gov/2020008882
LC ebook record available at https://lccn.loc.gov/2020008883

Printed in the United States of America
Mankato, MN
012021

ABOUT THE AUTHOR

Kelsey Jopp is an editor, writer, and lifelong learner. She lives in Maple Grove, Minnesota, where she enjoys practicing yoga and playing endless fetch with her sheltie, Teddy.

TABLE OF CONTENTS

CHAPTER 1
Welcome to Africa 5

CHAPTER 2
History of Africa 9

CHAPTER 3
Geography and Climate 15

LANDMARK PROFILE
The Nile River 18

CHAPTER 4
Plants and Animals 21

LANDMARK PROFILE
The Ituri Forest 26

CHAPTER 5
Natural Resources and Economy 29

CHAPTER 6
Government and Politics 35

CHAPTER 7
People and Culture 41

Focus on Africa • 46
Glossary • 47
To Learn More • 48
Index • 48

CHAPTER 1

WELCOME TO AFRICA

Africa sits between the Atlantic and Indian Oceans. In some areas, rain falls on dense forests. In others, desert land stretches on for miles. Some people catch fish on the coasts. Others go to jobs in bustling cities. Africa has more countries than any other continent. It covers nearly 12 million square miles (30 million sq km). That makes it the second-largest continent on Earth. Only Asia is larger.

People move through an urban market in southwestern Nigeria.

To study Africa, experts split the continent into five regions. They are Central Africa, East Africa, North Africa, Southern Africa, and West Africa. In all these regions, Africa is home to some of the world's fastest-growing cities. Johannesburg and Cape Town are in South Africa. Johannesburg built its wealth from mining gold. Cape Town is known for tourism and shopping. Other large cities include Cairo, Egypt, and Casablanca, Morocco. These cities are financial centers in North Africa.

Ghana, Liberia, and Nigeria are in West Africa. Lagos, Nigeria, is one of the largest African cities by population. In East Africa, there are Ethiopia, Kenya, and Somalia. Addis Ababa is Ethiopia's capital and home to the African Union's headquarters. Countries in Central Africa include Chad and Cameroon. Douala, Cameroon, is an industrial center with many factories.

Africa is also known for its physical features. There's the Nile River, the Sahara Desert, and the African rainforests. These features show how big and varied Africa really is. No two parts are alike.

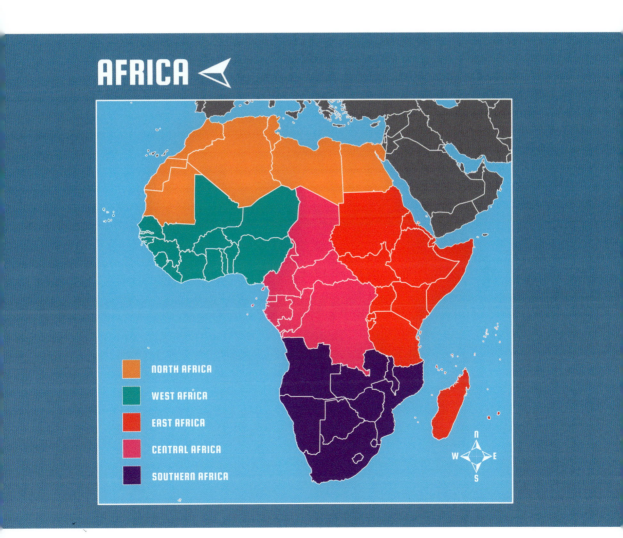

CHAPTER 2

HISTORY OF AFRICA

Africa was home to the first humans on Earth. At least 200,000 years ago, people hunted and gathered across the continent. As early as 11,000 years ago, people began farming. Over time, some groups became more complex. One example is ancient Egypt. Egyptians settled along the Nile River. Their **culture** thrived from 3100 to 332 BCE. It made great advances in science, art, and religion.

Between 2550 and 2490 BCE, ancient Egyptians built the Pyramids of Giza.

Other African cultures thrived as well. The Kingdom of Kush peaked in the 1000s BCE. This kingdom covered much of present-day Sudan. It was Egypt's trading partner and military rival.

Around the same time, the Bantu **migration** began. Bantu people traveled from West Africa to Central, Southern, and East Africa. This migration lasted more than 1,000 years. By the 100s CE, Bantu groups covered much of the southern half of Africa. They brought new tools and skills.

West Africa had other important resources. In the 100s CE, West African kingdoms began trading huge amounts of gold. They traded for salt from North Africa. In the 1100s, trading also grew on the Swahili coast. Swahili people descended from East African Bantu people. They traded iron, ivory, and animal products. They received jewelry, cloth, and texts.

In the 1400s, the transatlantic slave trade began. Europeans brutally enslaved West African people. They took captives to Europe. Soon, they expanded the slave trade to the Americas.

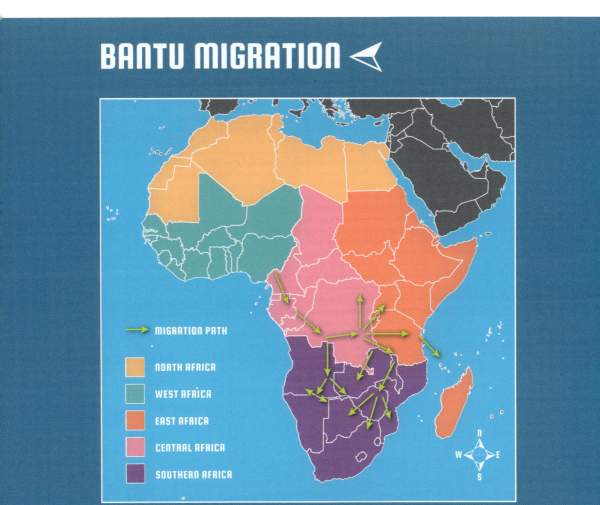

The slave trade finally ended in the late 1800s. By then, countries in the Americas and Europe had forced millions of African people across the Atlantic. This population loss was devastating. Many African societies struggled to keep developing.

Europe wanted the resources Africa held. Between 1870 and 1900, European powers **colonized** most of Africa. Many Africans resisted. Ethiopian troops, for example, defeated Italian forces in 1896. Even so, colonization caused a huge loss of resources for Africans. It made African political systems unstable. It also harmed many African people and cultures.

European control weakened after World War II (1939–1945). Many independent countries formed. This process was sometimes peaceful and other times violent. The **Cold War** also affected

▲ Nelson Mandela helped end South African apartheid, a system of racist segregation. Apartheid ended in 1994.

decolonization. The United States and its allies wanted to stop the spread of **Communism**. The Soviet Union and its allies wanted to spread it. Both sides supported conflicts that disrupted many African nations. The disruption was economic, political, and social.

Even so, many nations banded together during the Cold War. They formed the Organization of African Unity. This group worked to help African lives. In 2002, it became the African Union.

CHAPTER 3

GEOGRAPHY AND CLIMATE

The equator runs across the middle of Africa. North and south of the equator are the tropics. This warm, humid region stretches all around the world. Due to Africa's location, most of the continent is tropical. However, it is home to a variety of other climates as well.

Geographers often split Africa into eight physical regions. Each area features different climates. In the north lies the Sahara Desert.

The Congo basin is one of Earth's largest river basins. It runs along the equator in Central Africa.

15

▲ Simien National Park is part of the Ethiopian Plateau.

The Sahara is the world's largest hot desert. Below the Sahara is the Sahel. This is a stretch of flat plains. The savanna comes next, making up most of Central Africa. These grasslands stretch across nearly half the continent. Africa's rainforests are also in Central Africa.

On the east coast are the Ethiopian Plateau and the East African lakes. These regions surround a series of trenches called the Great East African Rift Valley. The Swahili coast is also in the east, along the Indian Ocean. Last is Southern Africa, made up of rocky plateaus and mountains.

Africa also has many water features. The Atlantic Ocean runs along the continent's western coast. The northern and eastern coasts are bordered by the Mediterranean Sea, Red Sea, and Indian Ocean. Africa's most notable water feature is the Nile River. This major source of water helps support the millions of people living on its shores.

Climate change is one of the greatest threats facing Africa today. Earth's rising temperature is negatively affecting rainfall. Many African societies depend on rain to grow food. But too much rain can cause floods. Due to climate change, sometimes there is too much rain. Other times, there is too little. It will take a global effort to slow climate change. Otherwise, Africa's people, land, and animals will suffer.

LANDMARK PROFILE

THE NILE RIVER

The Nile is one of the longest rivers in the world. It passes through 11 countries. For thousands of years, people have lived along the Nile. They use the river for fishing, farming, and transportation. Today, more than 200 million people depend on the river for water and food. However, the way one country uses the river can affect how other countries can use the river. For this reason, the river causes both cooperation and conflict among nations.

The Nile is made up of two smaller rivers. The White Nile and the Blue Nile meet up in the country of Sudan. Then they flow north, through Egypt, to the Mediterranean Sea. The area where the river meets the sea is called the Nile delta. Approximately half of Egypt's population is settled in this area.

▲ The Nile River flows for approximately 4,132 miles (6,650 km).

The Nile is home to a variety of animals. One of the most well-known is the Nile crocodile. This reptile can grow to be 20 feet (6.1 m) long. Nile crocodiles are very dangerous. They kill as many as 200 people each year.

Other animals along the Nile include the rhinoceros and baboon. The African tiger fish and vundu catfish swim in the Nile's waters. The tiger fish uses razor-sharp teeth to catch birds in flight.

CHAPTER 4

PLANTS AND ANIMALS

Because of Africa's diverse climates, the continent is home to a variety of animals. For example, only certain animals and plants can survive in the desert. One is the Arabian camel. This camel has a hump that holds fat. The camel breaks down the fat into water when it needs it. This adaptation helps the camel survive in the desert. People often use camels to move goods across the desert.

An Arabian camel's hump can hold up to 80 pounds (36 kg) of fat.

21

Due to harsh conditions, only certain plants can live in the desert. In parts of the Sahara, there are no plants at all. The plants that do survive must have deep roots. These roots can reach as deep as 80 feet (24 m). They gather water deep below the surface.

In the Sahel, animals compete for scarce food and water. The Senegal gerbil eats 10 percent of the region's plants. Many other plants are harvested by farmers. Two species of trees provide food for cattle. Acacia trees have deep roots that help them survive. And baobab trees have wide, sturdy trunks.

The Ethiopian Plateau is a mountain region in East Africa. Animals in this region must be quick and light. These traits help them move across the rocky landscape. The walia ibex is a type of wild goat that is native to the region. The Ethiopian

▲ Some baobab trees live for more than 2,000 years.

wolf lives there as well. The plateau is also home to the Ethiopian rose. This flower is Africa's only native rose species.

Many large mammals roam Africa's savannas. The Serengeti is Africa's most well-known savanna. Lions, giraffes, elephants, and zebras can be found here. Each year, wildebeests migrate across the area. They eat and stomp on the grass.

Their waste provides nutrients to the soil. In these ways, wildebeests help new grass grow.

The East African lakes are home to hippos and crocodiles. And in Southern Africa, there are many animal **reserves**. Southern African reserves offer protection to lions, elephants, white rhinos, and more. The Cape Floristic Region is also in Southern Africa. This is one of the richest plant areas in the world. It contains 20 percent of Africa's plant species.

Africa's rainforests are habitats for many plants and animals. Scientists have identified only 10 percent of the plant species in the rainforest.

➤ THINK ABOUT IT

What traits might help African animals survive in the desert? What about animals in the rainforest?

▲ The mountain gorilla is one of the closest living relatives to humans.

Some plant and animal species can only be found in Africa. One example is the mountain gorilla. This great ape lives in high-elevation forests of Rwanda, Uganda, and the Democratic Republic of the Congo.

Madagascar is also known for its plants and animals. This island-nation is located off the eastern coast of Africa. Approximately 90 percent of its species live nowhere else on Earth.

LANDMARK PROFILE

THE ITURI FOREST

The Ituri Forest lies in the Democratic Republic of the Congo. This rainforest is near the country's northeastern edge. Because it is so close to the equator, the Ituri Forest is tropical. One incredible feature of the Ituri Forest is its trees. Some trees grow to be 170 feet (52 m) tall. Due to the trees' many leaves, very little light reaches through to the forest floor.

The Ituri Forest is home to a huge variety of species. Hundreds of bird species make their homes there. Forest elephants and forest buffalo roam. In addition, the okapi is native to the Ituri Forest. This animal is related to the giraffe. But an okapi's legs have black-and-white stripes like a zebra. These stripes help okapis survive in the dark Ituri Forest. Young okapis can see their mothers' stripes well.

▲ Four Bambuti populations live in the Ituri Forest. These peoples are the Mbuti, Aka, Sua, and Efe.

People also live in the Ituri Forest. Pygmy peoples hunt and gather. The populations in the forest are known as the Bambuti. They live in groups of up to 100 people. These clans move frequently to find the best food. Music and dance are central parts of Bambuti life. In addition to the Bambuti, people such as the Bila live in villages. These people farm. The Bambuti and village dwellers trade labor and resources. They work together to share the forest.

CHAPTER 5

NATURAL RESOURCES AND ECONOMY

Africa has many resources that contribute to the continent's economies. One of its major economic activities is agriculture. More than 60 percent of the population depends on subsistence farming. Farmers grow food to feed their families. They sell few or none of their crops. Many people also raise livestock, including cattle, sheep, and goats. Family members, and women in particular, do much of this work.

Herders travel with their cattle in western Nigeria.

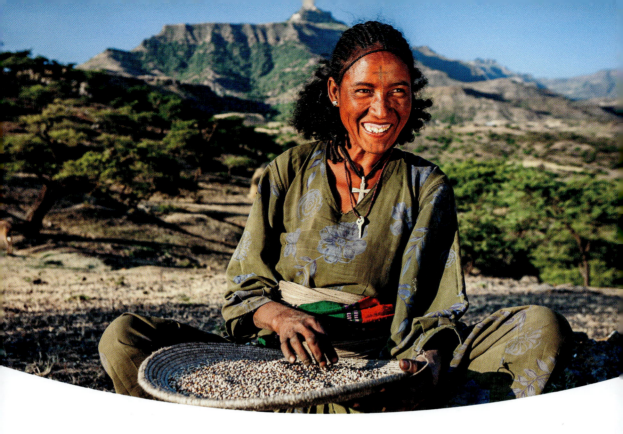

▲ A woman sifts sorghum in northern Ethiopia.

Crops vary depending on the region. Common crops across Africa include plantains, peanuts, eggplants, and peppers. In Ethiopia, the economy depends heavily on farming. Top crops include teff, wheat, sorghum, and barley.

South Africa also boasts a variety of crops, such as tomatoes, corn, onions, pumpkins, and carrots. These crops were all introduced from overseas. In fact, only three of the continent's top vegetables are native to Africa. These crops are cowpeas, yams, and okra.

Other major economic activities are **forestry**, fishing, mining, and drilling. Forests are common in Central and West Africa. Countries in these regions depend on forestry for much of their wealth. Certain expensive woods grow across Central Africa. These include mahogany and okoume. African countries sell these woods to countries in Europe and Asia.

Coastal regions often rely on fishing. West Africa produces huge amounts of fish each year. It has one of the world's top fishing industries. Large fish, such as tuna and cod, bring in the most money. However, people mainly catch smaller fish. These fish include sardines and herring.

Many people fish in Africa's lakes and rivers as well. But these people tend not to sell their fish outside Africa. Instead, local people consume much of the fish from lakes and rivers.

Much of Africa's wealth comes from its mineral resources. The continent is rich in gold, diamonds, and more. Nearly half of Africa's gold production is in South Africa. This nation also produces many diamonds. Due to its natural resources, South Africa was the continent's second-largest economy in 2019. Other top diamond producers in Africa are Botswana, Angola, and the Democratic Republic of the Congo. Together, Africa produces half of the world's diamonds.

Africa also gains wealth through fuel production. Countries around the world invest money in Africa's stores of oil and gas. The majority of oil and gas reserves are in North and

▲ A miner readies drilling machinery in South Africa's South Deep gold mine.

West Africa. Nigeria's oil supply helped make it the continent's largest economy as of 2019.

Other top economic activities in Africa are tourism and manufacturing. Egypt makes most of its wealth from these activities. It was Africa's third-largest economy in 2019. Morocco has another large economy. Tourism and manufacturing have helped the nation grow.

33

CHAPTER 6

GOVERNMENT AND POLITICS

Africa has a variety of government systems. Most African nations are republics. This kind of government is run by elected officials that represent the public. There are different types of republics. Many African nations are presidential republics. The president is separate from the lawmaking part of the government. This leader carries out laws. Examples of presidential republics are Angola, Rwanda, and Cameroon.

Rwanda's president, Paul Kagame, meets with the European Union in 2018.

There are also parliamentary republics. These kinds of nations include Botswana and South Africa. There, a parliament selects the executive leaders. The parliament makes the nation's laws.

A few African governments are monarchies. Monarchs gain their positions due to their family lines. Examples of monarchies are Lesotho, Morocco, and Eswatini (also known as Swaziland). In Lesotho, the king does not have executive or lawmaking powers. In Eswatini, the king has total control.

Today, many African governments face conflict and change. For example, a civil war has divided Somalia since 1991. Between 1991 and 2020, millions of Somali people fled their homes. During this war, a militant group formed. It committed acts of **terrorism** throughout East Africa. Terrorism causes political unrest across West

▲ People in Tunisia protest their leader during the beginning of the Arab Spring in 2011.

Africa, too. Militant groups make governments across East and West Africa unstable.

In many nations, civilians fought to change their governments. The Arab Spring is a major example. In the early 2010s, people started uprisings across North Africa and the Middle East. People overthrew **authoritarian** governments in Tunisia, Egypt, and Libya. Tunisia's first truly democratic election took place in 2011.

▲ Women largely led the 2019 revolution in Sudan.

Other nations were not as successful. The uprisings led to civil war in Libya.

Other protests began later. In 2016, people in Zimbabwe started to protest their leader. Robert Mugabe had held office for nearly four decades. In 2017, the country's military took charge. Mugabe resigned. Even so, political unrest continued.

In 2018, years of protest caused Ethiopia's leader to step down. The new prime minister, Abiy Ahmed, made huge changes. For example, Ahmed freed Ethiopia's political prisoners. He also helped end a 20-year border conflict with Eritrea.

In April 2019, Sudanese people overthrew their longtime ruler. The military took over. Protesters wanted civilians to have power. In August 2019, the two groups agreed to a transition plan.

Several African governments have been models for peace. These nations include Ghana, Mauritius, Senegal, Cape Verde, South Africa, and Botswana. A democratic government has led Ghana since 1992. Botswana has been democratic since its independence in 1966. It has the longest multiparty democracy in Africa.

THINK ABOUT IT ◁

The Arab Spring led to both success and war. What do you think makes a protest successful?

CHAPTER 7

PEOPLE AND CULTURE

More than 1.3 billion people live in Africa. As a result, its people and cultures are incredibly diverse. Between 1,000 and 2,000 languages are spoken on the continent. During colonization, countries often had to adopt European languages. But most people also speak local languages. In some cases, people combined African and European languages. For instance, Ghanaian English has words unique to Ghana.

Swahili is the most-spoken language in Africa, especially in East African countries like Tanzania.

The world's 20 most diverse nations are in Africa. Uganda is the most diverse. More than 40 ethnic groups live in Uganda alone. These groups include the Ganda, Iteso, and Soga. Each group has its own language and culture. For instance, the Ganda people have produced cloth made from bark for thousands of years. They use a technique older than weaving.

Colonization continues to affect African cultures. In South Africa, there are the Afrikaners. This white ethnic group is descended from Dutch colonizers of the 1600s. For years, the group dominated the region. As a result, many South Africans had to adopt European culture. For example, most Zulu people in South Africa practice Christianity.

At the same time, many Zulu people have combined their traditional religion with

▲ Zulu people perform traditional Zulu music during a Christian service.

Christianity. For instance, Zulu religion focuses on ancestors. Ancestors remain an important part of Zulu Christianity. Other Zulu people honor their culture through music. Mbube is a form of modern Zulu music. It features choral harmonies. Mbube has a softer style called isicathamiya. This form of music has influenced music around the world.

▲ Nigeria is home to many musicians who are popular worldwide, including the artist Burna Boy.

Some groups live traditionally. In East Africa, there are the Hadza people of Tanzania. They are some of the last people to live as hunter-gatherers. However, Hadza life is changing. Most children attend school for a few years. Some wear Western clothes or own cell phones.

Many Yoruba people also carry on their traditions. They are known for their "talking" drums. They change the rhythm and pitch to make the drums represent words. Today, the Yoruba are one of the largest ethnic groups in Africa.

Many live in Lagos, Nigeria. Others still practice subsistence farming in rural areas of West Africa.

Some regions have been impacted by migration. For example, North African cultures were influenced by migration from the Middle East. Many people in North Africa speak a form of Arabic. Islam is also widespread.

Many people in Africa do not live in the country they were born in. Some moved to escape political conflict. Others moved for work opportunities. Due to high migration rates, African cultures are constantly changing. Africa will remain a diverse place that is rich with history, culture, and people.

THINK ABOUT IT ◀

Ethnic groups are important social units in many African communities. What social units are important in your community?

FOCUS ON
AFRICA

Write your answers on a separate piece of paper.

1. Write a paragraph that summarizes the key ideas of Chapter 6.

2. Africa is made up of many cultures that undergo constant change. What changes have you noticed in your own culture?

3. In which region of Africa is the Swahili coast located?
>   **A.** Southern Africa
>   **B.** East Africa
>   **C.** West Africa

4. Why has the civil war in Somalia caused so many people to flee their homes?
>   **A.** Many people left their homes to train for the war.
>   **B.** Many people left their homes to find a safe place to live.
>   **C.** Many people left their homes because the government told them to leave.

Answer key on page 48.

GLOSSARY

authoritarian
Putting the authority of the state above the freedoms of the people.

climate change
A human-caused global crisis involving long-term changes in Earth's temperature and weather patterns.

Cold War
A conflict of ideals between the United States and the Soviet Union that took place during the second half of the 1900s.

colonized
Established control over an area and the people who live there.

Communism
A political system in which all property is owned by the government.

culture
The way a group of people live; their customs, beliefs, and laws.

forestry
The activity of planting and managing areas of trees.

migration
When humans move from one region to another.

reserves
Areas of land that are protected to keep animals and plants safe.

terrorism
The use of violence to create fear in a group of people in order to achieve a political goal.

TO LEARN MORE

BOOKS

Harris, Duchess, and Marcia Amidon Lusted. *The Transatlantic Slave Trade*. Minneapolis: Abdo Publishing, 2020.

Heale, Jay, Yong Jui Lin, and Debbie Nevins. *Democratic Republic of the Congo*. New York: Cavendish Square, 2019.

Montgomery, Sy. *The Magnificent Migration: On Safari with Africa's Last Great Herds*. Boston: Houghton Mifflin Harcourt, 2019.

NOTE TO EDUCATORS

Visit **www.focusreaders.com** to find lesson plans, activities, links, and other resources related to this title.

INDEX

Angola, 32, 35

Botswana, 32, 36, 39

Cameroon, 6, 35

Democratic Republic of the Congo, 25, 26, 32

Egypt, 6, 9–10, 18, 33, 37

Ethiopia, 6, 12, 30, 38–39

Ghana, 6, 39, 41

Libya, 37–38

Madagascar, 25

Morocco, 6, 33, 36

Nigeria, 6, 33, 37, 45

Senegal, 39

Somalia, 6, 36

South Africa, 6, 30, 32, 36, 39, 42

Sudan, 10, 18, 39

Tunisia, 37

Uganda, 25, 42

Zimbabwe, 38

Answer Key: **1.** Answers will vary; **2.** Answers will vary; **3.** B; **4.** B